PAMPHLETS ON AMERICAN WRITERS • NUMBER 23

UNIVERSITY OF MINNESOTA

⤺ *Nathaniel Hawthorne*

BY HYATT H. WAGGONER

UNIVERSITY OF MINNESOTA PRESS • MINNEAPOLIS

Printed in the United States of America at
the Jones Press, Inc., Minneapolis

Library of Congress Catalog Card Number: 62-63701

Distributed to high schools in the United States by
McGraw-Hill Book Company, Inc.
New York   Chicago   Corte Madera, Calif.   Dallas

PUBLISHED IN GREAT BRITAIN, INDIA, AND PAKISTAN BY THE OXFORD
UNIVERSITY PRESS, LONDON, BOMBAY, AND KARACHI, AND IN
CANADA BY THOMAS ALLEN, LTD., TORONTO

NATHANIEL HAWTHORNE

HYATT H. WAGGONER is a professor of American literature at Brown University and chairman of the American Civilization Program there. He is the author of
Hawthorne: A Critical Study as well as other books of
literary criticism.

Nathaniel Hawthorne

WHEN Hawthorne was born in Salem, Massachusetts, in 1804 the town was already very old by American standards. The Hathornes had been there from the beginning. (Hawthorne added the *w* to the family name when he began to sign his stories.) By the 1690's one of them was prominent enough to be a judge in the witchcraft trials. His descendant's remarks on him in "The Custom House" Introduction to *The Scarlet Letter* mix pride in his prominence and a sense of inherited guilt for his deeds as judge.

Hawthorne is being a little whimsical in "The Custom House," protectively light in his tone, when he takes the judge's guilt on himself and offers to do penance that the family curse may be removed. But there is an undercurrent of seriousness. Salem is a part of him, for good and for ill. The "mere sensuous sympathy of dust for dust" is perhaps all that is needed to bind town and man together. Like William Faulkner in a later century, like Quentin remembering the tales out of the past in *Absalom, Absalom!* Hawthorne admits to being haunted by the figure of the prominent but guilty ancestor who "was present to my boyish imagination, as far back as I can remember."

Later Hathornes were neither so prominent nor so conspicuously guilty. While Salem grew and prospered, they sank into that "dreary and unprosperous condition" Hawthorne hopes, in "The Custom House," may be alleviated by his public assumption of the family guilt. When Captain Nathaniel Hathorne, a shipmaster, died on one of his voyages the year that young Nathaniel was four, the family decline was complete. Left without resources,

5

Elizabeth Manning Hathorne moved with her three children into the nearby home of her brother.

As he grew up, Hawthorne watched Salem decline. The Embargo of 1807 struck the town a heavy blow, and when the end of the War of 1812 made shipping possible again, Salem did not recover its importance as a seaport. The town was repeating the family history, it seemed. It was perhaps too late for both town and family. In his first work of fiction, which Hawthorne compounded of about equal portions of undigested, undistanced personal feelings and experience, and the conventions of the Gothic novel, the central figure, Fanshawe, thinks of himself as nobility in decline. He anticipates, and experiences, an early death. Late in life Hawthorne tried repeatedly to write a romance about an American claimant to a lost great English estate. With a part of himself at least, he was that claimant, as he was also Fanshawe.

When he graduated from Bowdoin in 1825, with *Fanshawe* already complete or nearly so, Hawthorne was determined to become a writer of fiction. Composition was the only subject in which he had excelled in college, or in which he had showed any great interest, and now he proposed to teach himself to write by writing. He spent the next dozen years in the now famous third-floor chamber of his uncle's house on Herbert Street in Salem, reading, writing, projecting volumes of tales refused by publishers, and, during the latter part of the period, publishing regularly in magazines and Christmas gift books or annuals. But the rate of pay for the stories was very low, and though he had increasing success in placing his work, he found himself unable to make even a modest living as a writer of tales.

In 1837 a friend secretly paid for the publication of *Twice-Told Tales*. This brought him a little group of admiring readers but no income. As an expedient, he undertook editorial work in Boston, then got a job in the Boston Custom House, and finally joined the Brook Farm community, hoping, apparently, that in that socialist society he would be able to combine the practical and the creative. But hard daily labor and social evenings left him neither energy nor time for writing, and after little more than a year there he left without regret and poorer than when he had joined.

At the age of thirty-eight Hawthorne married Sophia Peabody of the famous Salem family, and the next several years, spent in the Old Manse in Concord, were the happiest in his life. Here he partly wrote and partly collected from magazines which had published his work earlier the tales and sketches to make a second volume, *Mosses from an Old Manse.* Emerson, Thoreau, and Ellery Channing were friendly neighbors. With Channing Hawthorne boated on the river that flowed beside the house, as he tells us in "The Old Manse." It seemed, for a while, not unfitting to play with the notion that he and Sophia were a "New Adam and Eve."

But he was haunted from the beginning by a sense that this idyll could not last, and his fears, as was so often the case, proved to be well founded. With unpaid bills mounting steadily, and the owner giving notice that he wanted the Old Manse back for his own use, the family was forced to return to Salem, where Hawthorne took the job in the Custom House described in the Introduction to *The Scarlet Letter.* Fired from this position for political reasons, he turned back to his craft and wrote his greatest romance. As he worked on it, anxiety about money was still severe and grief at the death of his mother was intense, but he never again wrote so rapidly or so surely, or so much from the depths of his sensibility.

In this tale set in Puritan Boston, Hawthorne created four unforgettable characters of American fiction: Hester Prynne, condemned to wear a scarlet A on her breast in token of her sin of adultery; the Reverend Arthur Dimmesdale, revered as saintly by his parishioners but torn by hidden guilt; their child, the " 'Pearl' . . . of great price"; and Roger Chillingworth, Hester's husband, who as he probes into the hearts of those who have wronged him, becomes the greatest sinner of them all. The identity of Hester's lover, a secret her ministerial inquisitors cannot force her to reveal, is at last made public in a way the community could not have foreseen and would not have wished.

The Scarlet Letter established Hawthorne's reputation and made it possible, it seemed, for him to devote himself entirely to his writing. Settling in Lenox in the Berkshires, he quickly wrote *The House of the Seven Gables* and several works for children, a type of writing he found pleasant, easy, and comparatively profitable. Here he became a friend of Herman Melville, who was at work nearby on *Moby Dick*, which he later dedicated to Hawthorne. The cursed Hathornes became the cursed Pyncheons in *The House of the Seven Gables*, declining from wealth and prominence to poverty and eccentricity. Their claim to a great estate cannot be established, for the deed has been lost, as the actual deed to land in Maine was lost to Hawthorne's branch of his family. The many-gabled mansion images the family history: since it will not yield up its secrets for the guilt to be purged, it must be left behind by the new generation.

Mountain scenery and the simple life in the "little red farmhouse" finally palled, and the Hawthornes — there were now three children, Una, Julian, and Rose — returned to Concord to buy The Wayside from Amos Bronson Alcott. Then, when *The Blithedale Romance*, in temper and theme an anti-utopian reflection of the Brook Farm experience, failed to please Hawthorne's newly won public, and when the election of his college classmate and friend Franklin Pierce to the presidency opened the opportunity for a really remunerative political job, he accepted the

8

consulship in Liverpool. The following half-dozen years were uncreative ones. Though he worked sporadically at his writing, it was not until the end of the period that, by a sustained effort, he was able to write his last completed romance, *The Marble Faun*, in which an innocent young man falls into sin and rises into maturity.

When the family returned to America in 1860, Hawthorne had just four troubled years left. The European experience had proved valuable and pleasant, but it had not, as he had hoped it would, made him financially secure. Further, he found himself disliking the American climate and missing his English friends. Settling in Concord was, he began to think, a mistake. The Wayside — and Concord itself — did not seem like home to him, and as he thought of the many places the family had lived, he wondered if he could truthfully be said ever to have had a "home."

Working harder and more steadily on his writing now than he ever had for any extended period before, he was unable to bring any work of fiction to completion. Familiar scenes and symbolic images were reused, but in the margins of his manuscripts he wrote himself notes asking "What meaning?" His health began to fail and, haunted by a premonition of early death, he drove himself to write that he might at least leave his family provided for. Though the romances refused to take shape, the sketches of English life that came out as *Our Old Home* showed that he could still write trenchantly and beautifully on subjects that did not demand exploration of the depths of his imagination.

Provincial Salem and the secluded years of the long apprenticeship were now far in the past, and he had almost succeeded in becoming the "man of society" he had always wanted to be. His publishers pressed him for new work, and recognition of his achievement was widespread and gratifying. Now at least there was no outward reason for his recurrent dream of failure. But his ambivalence of mood increased until everything was Janus-faced. Much that we should like to know about these last years must remain speculative. We do not even know, for instance, what disease he was suffering from, whether physical or psycho-physical. Oliver Wendell Holmes examined him but could arrive at no sure diagnosis. The evidence for any conclusion is largely missing, but what there is of it seems to me to point to psychoso-matic changes.

One thing seems clear, though, if not the disease that aged him so suddenly and brought death at the age of sixty. The manu-scripts of the romances he could not complete suggest that the convictions that had once sustained him, providing a tolerable margin of clarity and meaning in a dark and ambiguous world, were now no longer operative, even if, in some sense, still held. "What meaning?"

When he died in 1864 in Plymouth, New Hampshire, on a trip with former President Pierce intended to benefit his health, he was far from home both literally and symbolically — far, in those days, from The Wayside in Concord, and farther still from that home of the heart's desire, that Eden that had been lost so long ago.

Hawthorne has remained an enigma to his biographers. Those who concentrate on the facts of the outward life tend to present a thoroughly normal and well-adjusted Hawthorne. They show us a man who liked to smoke cigars and drink brandy while playing cards. This Hawthorne may have seemed shy to Emerson but he enjoyed an easy friendship with less intellectual friends like Horatio Bridge and Franklin Pierce. It is quite true that to most of those whose impressions have come down to us he seemed re-served but not unusually withdrawn, thoughtful but certainly not depressed or melancholy. Indeed a good part of the record suggests that many found him ordinarily cheerful and sociable.

But this picture begins to waver and blur as soon as we turn from the remarks of observers to the inner life as revealed in the writing. The well-adjusted Hawthorne, we begin to suspect, is the man he would have liked to be, and no doubt partly succeeded in being, but it is not the man he knew from within. The letters, the *Notebooks*, and the more personal sketches all reveal a quite different man behind the social mask.

With varying degrees of disguise and aesthetic distance from his personal situation, the sketches in particular can take us into the imagination of the man who wrote the major works. "The Devil in Manuscript" is almost autobiography, while Hawthorne appears in "Earth's Holocaust" only as a naive young man who needs to be guided into an understanding of life's complexities. "The Journal of a Solitary Man," which is neither so literally informative as "The Devil in Manuscript" nor so distanced as "Earth's Holocaust," reveals a good deal of the inner Hawthorne whose existence casual observers did not often guess.

The sketch of the "solitary man" reveals not facts so much as attitudes. The years of Hawthorne's "solitary" apprenticeship, after his graduation from college and before his marriage, were not nearly so solitary as they seemed, both at the time and in retrospect. But the important thing is precisely how they *seemed* to the man who wrote so often of alienation. They seemed years of imprisonment in the solitude of self.

Hawthorne pictures the solitary man as "walking in the sunshine . . . yet cold as death." The young unfortunate suffers often from a "deep gloom sometimes thrown over his mind by his reflections on death." He longs to break out of his isolation by travel: perhaps thus he will find something more real than his shadowy existence. But he gets no further from his native village than Hawthorne had gone at the time of writing the sketch. Instead, he spends much of his time looking at himself in the mirror and trying to understand the "pale beauty" he sees there.

There is some aesthetic distance here, to be sure. In part, Hawthorne is contributing to the tradition of the romantic hero as sad clown. But there is also self-revelation. The Hawthorne revealed is not the one family and friends thought they knew but a melancholy young Narcissus who often felt alone even in the midst of company and who was gravely dissatisfied with what he saw in the looking glass. He thought much of death, felt cold and guilty, and wrote "Alice Doane's Appeal."

This Hawthorne blamed himself for his detachment and wrote "The Christmas Banquet." He wished that he could relate to others more easily, that he were not so coldly rational and appraising: he cast cold-hearted scientists in the roles of villains. He worried often about whether being an artist might not have the effect of increasing his alienation. Certainly it required him to study people as objects to be manipulated on his fictional canvas. Might he not come to feel that they were as much *his* creatures as the characters in his book? Should art be thought of as a kind of black magic and the artist as a sort of magician, like the witch of old and the mesmerist of the present? "The Prophetic Pictures" and "The Old Apple Dealer" express his concern with the problem.

This Hawthorne felt guilty about being an artist and determined not to become a mesmerist. Though he toyed, at least once, with the thought that he might enjoy, for a while, being "a spiritualized Paul Pry, hovering invisible round man and woman, witnessing their deeds, searching into their hearts," he countered the temptation by writing so often of the hearth as a redemptive symbol that reference to it became a hallmark of his style. The hearth suggested all that the solitary man and the cold observer of Christmas festivities lacked: warmth and hope and fellow-feeling and the love that held together the family circle. Reunion after isolation came in his works to be both a symbol of and the literal means to salvation. No writer has ever placed a higher value on communion and community.

But he continued to note in himself, and to disapprove, feelings and attitudes he projected in Chillingworth and Rappaccini and Goodman Brown. He noted his tendency not only to study others with cold objectivity but to study himself with almost obsessive interest. He looked into the glass too often and searched too curiously the hearts of others: he wrote "Egotism, or the Bosom Serpent" and "Ethan Brand," condemning both protagonists, the first for his self-concern, the second for treating people as objects of study. Hawthorne had no admiration for detached observers, but he knew one well enough from within to be able to write about the type with authority.

"No human effort, on a grand scale, has ever yet resulted according to the purpose of its projectors. The advantages are always incidental. Man's accidents are God's purposes." Thus Hawthorne dismissed the moral significance of the Civil War. "Chiefly about War Matters," in which these aphorisms occur, is one of his last completed pieces of writing, done when his health was already failing and he was deeply distressed about the war itself. His political position as a Democrat, too, must have made it peculiarly difficult for him to clarify his feelings. We may be tempted to attribute the coldness of the remark, its implied disengagement from the human effort, to conditions of the moment.

But the idea was not new to Hawthorne. Years before, writing his campaign biography of Franklin Pierce, he had said the same thing: "There is no instance, in all history, of the human will and intellect having perfected any great moral reform by methods which it adapted to that end . . ." The idea was obviously a useful one in a defense of Pierce, a New Hampshire Democrat who needed the support of the South to be elected, but Hawthorne felt no need to invent it for the occasion. He found himself predisposed toward it by feelings that recurred throughout his life, whenever his supply of hope ran low.

The background of the idea is lighted up by a passage in *The English Notebooks* discussing his reluctance to give the advice his position as American consul in Liverpool seemed to require him to give. "For myself," he wrote, "I had never been in the habit of feeling that I could sufficiently comprehend any particular conjunction of circumstances with human character, to justify me in thrusting in my awkward agency among the intricate and unintelligible machinery of Providence. . . . It is only one-eyed people who love to advise, or have any spontaneous promptitude of action."

Hawthorne believed in Providence even while he found it unintelligible. Confronted with the problem of evil in the form of diseased and suffering English children, he concluded a *Notebook* entry with "Ah, what a mystery!" But he trusted there was a higher purpose, a final meaning in a dark and bewildering world, even if we could not clearly *know* it. "Man's accidents are God's purposes."

Hawthorne in short was a theist who thought of himself as a Christian, but he was skeptical of all claims, whether Puritan or Roman Catholic, to know the details of the divine will. Brought up a Unitarian, he associated himself with no church at all, yet preferred Bunyan to the religious liberals of his day and impressed family and friends as a religious man. He and Melville talked often, and with full mutual understanding, of "final things," but where Melville, like his own Ahab, was compelled to try to strike through the mask of appearance, Hawthorne could better abide the not knowing.

Nathaniel Hawthorne

Hawthorne's special mixture of skepticism and faith had much to do with the form of his art as well as his choice of themes. His clearest convictions tended to get expressed in allegory; his dimmer intimations, his hopes and fears, on the other hand, often found expression in tales more mythopoetic than allegorical, closer to modern symbolic fiction than to Bunyan. No less honest and courageous than Melville, he had a different temperament. He found he could live in the darkness with only a little light. Whatever else Hawthorne was, he was not one-eyed. Out of his ironic vision and his sense of paradox came most of his finest work.

Since ours is an age that has found irony, ambiguity, and paradox to be central not only in literature but in life, it is not surprising that Hawthorne has seemed to us one of the most *modern* of nineteenth-century American writers. The bulk and general excellence of the great outburst of Hawthorne criticism of the past decade attest to his relevance for us. It requires no distortion of him to see him not only as foreshadowing Henry James in his concern for "the deeper psychology" but as first cousin to Faulkner and Robert Penn Warren. In all the essentials, "My Kinsman, Major Molineux" is as "modern" a story as "The Bear." Hawthorne's themes, especially, link him with the writing and sensibility of our time.

Alienation is perhaps the theme he handles with greatest power. "Insulation," he sometimes called it — which suggests not only isolation but imperviousness. It is the opposite of that "osmosis of being" that Warren has written of, that ability to respond and relate to others and the world. Its causes are many and complex, its results simple: it puts one outside the "magic circle" or the "magnetic chain" of humanity, where there is neither love nor reality. It is Hawthorne's image of damnation. Reunion,

15

often imaged by the hearth, is his redemptive cure. Anticipating Archibald MacLeish of *J. B.*, he would have his characters "blow on the coal of the heart." Not "knowing" or "using" but "meeting" others — to borrow Martin Buber's terms — would offer a way back into the magic circle to alienated Chillingworth, Ethan Brand, or Rappaccini.

Contemporary critics have shown an even greater interest in Hawthorne's treatment of initiation. Though he wrote only a few stories directly concerned with it, several of them are among his greatest and a number of others touch it tangentially. Stories as rich, yet controlled, in meaning as "My Kinsman" are rare in this or any language. Initiated into life's complexity in a dreamlike evening in a strange city, the young man of the story achieves a difficult maturity. But the protagonist of "Young Goodman Brown" is unable to understand or accept the evil revealed to him in the forest of the soul, loses faith in the reality of the good, and lives the rest of his long life in gloomy alienation. The young couple in "The Maypole of Merrymount" are granted a happier outcome, but Giovanni in "Rappaccini's Daughter" is, like Goodman Brown, unable to accept life's ambiguous mixture of good and evil and so cannot understand his Beatrice or gain the salvation her love would grant.

When such initiations as these have happy outcomes, as in "My Kinsman," we are tempted to see them primarily in psychological terms, as dramatizing the process of maturation. When the results are less happy, so that we have a sense chiefly of the cost of losing innocence, we are likely to read them as versions of the Fall, the myth of the expulsion from the Garden. The psychological and the theological readings are perhaps just different ways of looking at the same archetypal story.

Hawthorne at any rate refused to simplify guilt by reducing it either to merely subjective and irrational "guilt feeling" or to wholly objective and external "sin." He concerned himself instead with guilt feelings that have personal and social causes and cures that are objectively real, not merely subjective or irrational, and that imply the reality of moral obligation. His special way of maintaining the ambiguous connection between the psychological, the moral, and the religious is one of the principal reasons why his works seem so relevant to us.

Moral and religious concerns, in short, are almost always central in Hawthorne's work, but Hawthorne's interest in them is primarily subjective and psychological. But his subjectivism is never solipsist and his psychologism never reductive. Rather, they are signs that his concern with matters moral and religious is existential. Like the Existentialist philosophers who articulate the sensibility of our time, Hawthorne is more concerned with the experienced toothache than with orthodontic theory. Like them he explores the nature of existential guilt, relating it to alienation, reunion, and commitment. Like them too he distrusts the claim of objective reason to be able to arrive at humanly relevant truth: his "empiricists" all end unhappily.

We may call such attitudes romantic rather than existential if we wish. Existential philosophy begins with Kierkegaard, in the romantic movement; but Kierkegaard seems more relevant to many today than John Dewey. Romanticism at this depth is still with us, and perhaps always will be, now that unquestioning certainty about life's "essences" seems unlikely ever to return. Not to be existential in the sense in which Hawthorne was is either to be content with positivism or to assume as unquestionable a fixed and absolute order of truth.

But if the first thing we should notice about Hawthorne is his "modernity," his immediate relevance to us and our concerns, the second thing, if we are to avoid the distortion of seeing in him

17

only our own image, is the way in which he is *not* one of us. It has been said that he was an eighteenth-century gentleman living in the nineteenth century, and the remark has enough truth in it to be useful to us at this point.

His style, for instance, though at its best a wonderfully effective instrument for the expression of his sensibility, is likely to strike us as not nearly so modern as Thoreau's. It was slightly old-fashioned even when he wrote it. It is very deliberate, with measured rhythms, marked by formal decorum. It is a public style and, as we might say, a "rhetorical" one — though of course all styles are rhetorical in one sense or another. It often prefers the abstract or generalized to the concrete or specific word. Compared to what the writers of handbooks, under the influence of modernist literature, have taught us to prefer — the private, informal, concrete, colloquial, imagistic — Hawthorne's style can only be called premodern.

But it is not only style in this narrow sense that marks Hawthorne as a nineteenth-century writer. Apart from that aspect of his writing that we may summarize under the general heading of his symbolism, his whole procedure as a fictionist is pre-modern — which is to say, pre-Flaubert and pre-James. He is one of the most regularly intrusive of intrusive authors. The basic rule of post-Jamesian fiction, reduced by handbook writers to a simple inviolable formula, has been "Don't tell, show!" Hawthorne both tells and shows — tells not simply in his characteristic final moral comment but all the way through.

Ethan Brand, for instance, seeing the absurdity of his situation, bursts into laughter. Hawthorne, having presented the image, then comments: "Laughter, when out of place, mistimed, or bursting forth from a disordered state of feeling, may be the most terrible modulation of the human voice." Hawthorne has lost something in immediacy, and gained something in meaning.

Later in the story, in his summary of Brand's career, he does not "show" at all, he merely tells: "Thus Ethan Brand became a fiend. He began to be so from the moment that his moral nature had ceased to keep the pace of improvement with his intellect." "He had lost his hold of the magnetic chain of humanity."

In its insistence that the author never appear in his own pages, that the image alone do all the work, modern fiction has paralleled Imagist poetry. Hawthorne knows nothing of this. For him, fiction was a way of exploring life to find meaning. Not being post-Jamesian, he thought he had a right to bring out and underline the meanings his images revealed. The classic forms of fiction had always permitted this.

If Hawthorne had thought he needed any excuse for his intrusive comments, he might well have said what Faulkner has said of *his* writing, that he wrote "to uplift men's hearts . . . [to] say No to death." Hawthorne wants to strengthen and encourage man, to help him to live in a world in which the ways of Providence are mostly unintelligible.

Since Melville first detected the darkness in Hawthorne's work and praised him for saying No in thunder, a great many sensitive readers have found the dark Hawthorne more impressive than the light. But this is not the way Hawthorne wanted to be, these not the meanings he intended.

The problem is a complex one, but in part it may be somewhat simplified by making two distinctions, the first between the artist and the man, the second between two types of meaning in the art. Hawthorne the artist often did his best writing when he wrote not of what he "believed," or wanted to believe, or thought he should believe, but of the "phantoms" that came unsought and "haunted" him. "The Haunted Mind" can give us the clue here. To the "passive sensibility" halfway between sleep and waking the spectral shapes of shame and death appear: when we get fully awake and the conscious mind takes control, they vanish. Much of Hawthorne's best writing comes out of the haunted mind.

But it is not pleasant or comfortable to be visited by such specters. Hawthorne had to live as a man as well as survive as an artist, and it may well be that one of the reasons he gave up writing short fiction after he had established himself as a writer is that so many of his best early tales *had* come from the depths of the mind — by a process he had no wish to repeat. Hawthorne's desire to be a well-adjusted "man of society" and his disinclination to reveal his inner life in public were in some degree in conflict with his desire to be an artist.

The distinction between the two types of meaning in his art takes us into an area somewhat less conjectural. The distinction I have in mind is that between intended and achieved meaning. Hawthorne hoped that *The Scarlet Letter* might have a happy ending, but the hope he expressed in his first chapter in connection with the rose blooming on the bush beside the prison — that it might lighten his dark tale — did not materialize, even for him. He resolved that his next novel would be a happier one.

The conflict here is only between the hope (or intention? — how consciously had Hawthorne thought out *The Scarlet Letter* before writing it?) of the man, and the achievement of the artist. There is no conflict in the novel, of the type that weakens a work, between intended and achieved meanings. The novel is all of a piece, with a magnificent unity of meaning that emerges equally from what it says and what it shows. But *The House of the Seven Gables* is perhaps not so perfect, for this reason among others. It is almost equally difficult to suppose that the ending was intended to be ironic and for the modern reader to take it any other way. And *The Blithedale Romance* was probably intended to mean only that utopian communities will not succeed unless their members have a change of heart and that frosty old bachelors like Coverdale need girls like Priscilla (or Sophia) to warm their hearts and give them hope. But what it actually means as a work of art is not so simply said, or so hopeful.

We may often, as we have seen, go to the sketches to find out the meanings Hawthorne *intended* to express in the fiction. In the sketches *belief* is generally in control, the phantoms that haunt the mind mostly absent; and Hawthorne's belief maintains a nice balance between the light and the dark. "Earth's Holocaust," for instance, tells us what Hawthorne must have intended to say on his theme of social reform in *Blithedale*. The sketch is one of Hawthorne's finest, and its structure is dramatic, so its meaning is not easily reduced to a brief summary. But a part of its meaning is this: reform is perennially needed, and we may well be grateful for many of the reforms of the past, but reform is superficial and impermanent unless it is accompanied by a change of heart. The source of evil is in the heart of man, not primarily in institutions. The devil laughs when man supposes that lasting progress toward the good can be brought about by merely external and social changes.

But if man's misguided efforts cause laughter in Hell, there is still hope, for if man will look deeper for the source of the evil he may find it. There is at any rate a guide for his efforts which he may use if he will. The attempt of the reformers to destroy the Bible as the climax of their enlightened reforms is unavailing. The fire, Hawthorne tells us, is powerless to consume it. Its pages even "assumed a more dazzling whiteness as the finger marks of human imperfection were purified away."

"Sunday at Home" maintains the same kind of balance between the light and the dark, negation and affirmation, that we find in "Earth's Holocaust." But since the language in which Hawthorne defines himself in the sketch as at once gentle skeptic and firm believer seems more dated than the language of the greater sketch, and since the meanings are less solidly embodied in dramatic images, "Sunday at Home" may reveal the balance Hawthorne intended to express better than the greater works do. It is more interesting as a piece of self-revelation than as a work of art.

Hawthorne begins by dissociating himself from the committed believers among his fellow townsmen. While they go to church, he stays at home and peeps at them through the window. He hears the bells but misses the sermon — and feels no loss. He finds aids to faith everywhere, not only in the sound of the bells. Even the sunshine seems to have a special "sabbath" quality about it. This last is no doubt an illusion, but such illusions, he believes, are often "shadows of great truths": "Doubts may flit around me, or seem to close their evil wings, and settle down; but, so long as I imagine that the earth is hallowed, and the light of heaven retains its sanctity, on the Sabbath — while that blessed sunshine lives within me — never can my soul have lost the instinct of its faith. If it have gone astray, it will return again."

The ideas being expressed here may strike us at first as just as archaic as the language. Nineteenth-century "religion of the heart" offers as little appeal today to the neo-orthodox as to the skeptical. But if we look again and note the meaning in the idea of a "hallowed" earth, we may find the notion not simply senti- mental. To find the earth itself holy is to find the sources of re- ligious faith in experience. The General Revelation — Nature — will then complement and reinforce the special, unique Revela- tion of Scripture. The idea is, we are likely to say too quickly, a romantic one; too quickly, because it is not only romantic but Scriptural, as we may see in the Psalms.

The sketch is light in tone and does not pretend to any pro- fundity, but it seems fair to say that Hawthorne is groping here toward a sacramental view of nature. He is no primitivist. He does not suppose that going "back to nature" will cure man's ills or automatically dispel all "evil" doubts. But he does think nature, as the handiwork of God, contains a general revelation of God's purposes and life's meaning, if we will only read it aright.

Religious faith, then, in this sketch, rests on our ability to experience the world in a certain way. And that way of experiencing is dependent on the imagination. When Hawthorne says "so long as I *imagine* that the earth is hallowed," he does not mean "so long as I *pretend*" or "so long as I *make believe*." He means that religion, like art, is visionary. This is the complement to his acknowledgment, in "Earth's Holocaust" and elsewhere, of the authority of a "purified" Scriptural revelation.

"Sunday at Home" maintains the kind of balance Hawthorne always wanted to keep and affirms the light in a way quite typical of him. It reveals a side of Hawthorne that Melville missed — or was not interested in — when he hailed the nay-sayer.

Writing in 1842 to the editor of *Sargent's New Monthly Magazine* about a sketch he hoped to place there, Hawthorne made a statement that, while it applies directly to the piece he had in mind, applies also, less directly and not intentionally, to all his fiction. "Whether it have any interest," he wrote, "must depend entirely on the sort of view taken by the writer, and the mode of execution."

As an artist, Hawthorne knew that in art the question is less *what* than *how*, that in a very important, though probably not absolute and exclusive sense, manner is more important than matter, the "fact" unimportant until transformed by "vision." Though he did not normally choose to exercise his talent or test his vision on trifles, he always insisted that the artist's *way of seeing* his subject was the important thing.

This insistence was, of course, both a permanent truth in art and a reflection of the romantic aesthetic, in which the artist is always peculiarly central. Just as clearly, it reflects an idealistic metaphysic. Not the thing known but the knowing, not matter but mind, is the locus of reality for idealism. Here Hawthorne and Emerson agreed. Whether or not Hawthorne should be called a "transcendentalist" depends on how one uses the term — broadly, to point to all varieties of transcendental philosophy, or narrowly, to designate the Concord New Thought. If broadly, then Plato was one of the first transcendentalists, and perhaps the most important; and Hawthorne was a somewhat uneasy and qualified one too. If narrowly, then Hawthorne was still in some respects a transcendentalist *malgré lui*, but it is important to remember that he thought of himself as not "tinged" with that radicalism.

In any case, however much he may have minimized, or been unaware of, his agreements with his neighbor. Emerson, Hawthorne believed that not only the finished work of art but reality itself depended on "the sort of view taken" by artist or man. The best sort of view would, he thought, be that which provided *distance* — in time or space — so that the raw fact as such could not dominate, so that irrelevant multiplicity would be dimmed and softened by distance to allow the pattern, the meaning, to emerge. Long views were best, just *because* the viewer could not see the details so well.

In view of this conviction, it is not hard to see why the past was so useful to him. The past was not only his South Seas, where romance was, but his relevant truth. We may see the consequences of such an aesthetic credo clearly enough in *The Scarlet Letter*. It is not the fact of adultery itself that engages Hawthorne's interest. Adultery might mean anything or nothing. Let it occur before the novel opens and explore its consequences. In Hawthorne's view it was personal guilt, not sin abstractly defined, that was interesting. This was one of the differences between him and his Puritan ancestors.

Writing the novel, Hawthorne took pains to supply just enough verisimilitude to make it credible. But for the most part he was simply not deeply concerned with merely external reality — except as that reality, perceived as symbol, could take us into the interiors of hearts and minds. That is why writing that must be classified as expository and descriptive (as compared with narrative) bulks so large in the work.

"The Old Apple Dealer" does not have even *The Scarlet Letter*'s minimum of action, but it illuminates what Hawthorne was about in his greatest novel. As a sketch rather than a tale, it is purely descriptive and expository: in it nothing happens except to the speaker, who gains a recognition which alters his point of view. There is even a sense in which the sketch is not "about" anything — or rather, in which it is about "nothing." It is for this reason that any interest it may have must come, as Hawthorne explained to the editor of *Sargent's*, from something other than the intrinsic interest of the subject itself.

For the old apple dealer who will be described is, Hawthorne says in the sketch, a purely negative character, featureless, colorless, inactive, hardly alive apparently. He seems an embodiment of torpor, an instance of nonentity. Such a subject is a challenge to the artist, and Hawthorne opens his sketch with a confession of his difficulty. How could one make interesting, or even imaginatively real, a subject intrinsically colorless and featureless? Hawthorne is not sure he can succeed, but he will try, for the very insignificance of the old man gives him a special kind of interest. "The lover of the moral picturesque may sometimes find what he seeks in a character which is nevertheless of too negative a description to be seized upon and represented to the imaginative vision by word painting."

That Hawthorne had indeed found in the old apple dealer what he sought as a lover of the "moral picturesque" is attested by the success of the sketch. For the subject allows Hawthorne to do several things at once. From one point of view, the sketch is about man's nothingness, and the significant qualification of that nothingness. From another, it is about the difficulties, opportunities, and dangers of the artist.

By the end, the difficulties have become opportunities — though Hawthorne does not claim so much — but the dangers remain. Against them Hawthorne issues a final warning that unites the two "subjects" of the sketch, art and life — issues it to himself most clearly, but to all artists by implication. The language of the ending is explicitly religious, but the aesthetic implications of it are clear enough.

Hawthorne had begun his sketch by telling us that without his subject's being aware of his scrutiny, he has "studied the old apple dealer until he has become a naturalized citizen of my inner world." Since what interests one in this "featureless" man is the perfection of his insignificance, if he is to come alive for readers, the artist will have to give him life. By what James would later call "the alchemy of art" he will be brought into being.

Power so great as this brings with it great danger. Hawthorne's metaphor for art in the sketch is witchcraft. Was art a kind of black magic? If the artist can legitimately claim his literary creations as entirely his own, may he not as man similarly conceive of other people as created — and perhaps controlled — by his knowing them? But if we think of other people as objects to be studied and manipulated, as Chillingworth thought of Dimmesdale and Ethan Brand thought of the subjects of his moral experiment, we shall be totally shut out from the saving realities of life. The fate to which the artist, like the scientist, Hawthorne felt, was peculiarly liable was alienation.

The assumption of Godlike knowledge could destroy
man equally. Knowledge brings with it the possibility o
and the artist must achieve control of his subject by con
his medium; but he will falsify reality if he omits the e..ment
of mystery and assumes that he knows the unknowable. One
error, then, to which the artist is peculiarly liable, threatens both
artist and man. But to see how Hawthorne prepares us to accept
his conclusion, which tests art by life's standards and sees life
through the eyes of the artist, we must return to Hawthorne's way
of bringing the old apple dealer to life in his pages.

Early in the sketch Hawthorne decides that with so negative a
subject the only way to describe him is to use negative compari-
sons, to tell us what he is *not* like. Perhaps in this way he will be
able to get at the paradox of a man who seemed completely inactive and stationary, yet whose immobility was composed of con-
tinuous minor, almost undetectible, movements. (So "stationary"
a man will never "go ahead," never join in "the world's exulting
progress.") Then the inspiration comes: what he is most of all *not*
like is the steam engine that roars at intervals through the station
where the old man sits so quietly. "I have him now. He and the
steam fiend are each other's antipodes . . ."

"I have him now." By using contrast the artist has succeeded in
conveying to us what he had almost despaired of conveying, the reality of a person who is almost nothing. But as soon as it is made,
the claim seems excessive: Hawthorne does not finally "know"
the old man at all, nor do we. For he has omitted something from
his description, something all-important that he has no way of
getting at — the soul. In a superficial sense he has succeeded: inso-
far as the old man is merely viewed, merely scrutinized, he is a
torpid machine in perfect contrast to the active, "progressive"
machine. But there is a deeper contrast involved than mere ac-
tivity or lack of it, and here the artist must confess the limits of

27

his art. "Could I read but a tithe of what is written . . . [in the old man's "mind and heart"] it would be a volume of deeper and more comprehensive import than all that the wisest mortals have given to the world; for the soundless depths of the human soul and of eternity have an opening through your breast. God be praised . . ."

So in the end Hawthorne makes his last confession: whatever his success in describing the old man behavioristically, he did *not* "have" him when he compared him, the stationary machine, to the steam engine, the active machine. Man cannot be fully known in the way we know a machine. This is the deeper sense in which the old man is the antipodes of the engine. To confuse the two is the ultimate error, for both artist and man.

"The Old Apple Dealer" emphasizes the creativity of the artist and the danger such creativity brings with it. The danger is partly that the artist will suppose that he *knows* more than he can possibly know. "Night Sketches: Beneath an Umbrella" dramatizes the danger of the artist's becoming so isolated from reality that his art will be a sort of daydream. Considered together, the two pieces imply that art is both a kind of knowledge — which must never pretend to finality, never lose its sense of mystery — and a kind of dream — which must keep in touch with reality. Art is more like myth than like document, but there are true myths and false myths, and art had better be true.

"Beneath an Umbrella" opens with a long paragraph devoted to describing the pleasures of the unrestricted imagination as it takes one on imaginary travels to exotic lands. "Pleasant is a rainy winter's day, within doors!" the speaker exclaims at the beginning, going on to explain that the "sombre" condition of the world outside the chamber window makes the exercise of unrestrained fancy all the more delightful by contrast. The warm, well-lighted chamber contains the whole world, so long as imagination is active.

Nevertheless, pleasant as daydreaming is, reality *will* break in: "the rain-drops will occasionally be heard to patter against my window panes . . ." As nightfall approaches, "the visions vanish, and will not come again at my bidding." Irresponsible dreaming, it would seem, finally ceases to be even pleasurable: "Then, it being nightfall, a gloomy sense of unreality depresses my spirits, and impels me to venture out, before the clock shall strike bedtime, to satisfy myself that the world is not entirely made up of such shadowy materials as have busied me throughout the day. A dreamer may dwell so long among fantasies, that the things without him will seem as unreal as those within."

About to step outside, the speaker pauses to "contrast the warmth and cheerfulness of my deserted fireside with the drear obscurity and chill discomfort" into which he is about to "plunge." The contrast contains, it becomes clear as the sketch goes on, nearly all of Hawthorne's favorite antinomies: the light and the dark; warmth and coldness, in the human heart as well as externally; faith and doubt; even, implicitly, the heart and the head, if we see here the meanings Hawthorne constantly implies elsewhere when he uses hearth and chamber as heart images. The sketch is rich in meaning. It contains, indeed, in epitome nearly all the central issues of Hawthorne's moral and religious thought, and it significantly illuminates a side of his aesthetic thinking it is easy to overlook.

On the doorstep now, the speaker asks the reader to pardon him if he has "a few misgivings." He is, he thinks, entitled to them, our "poor human nature" being what it is. And in view of what is about to be revealed about reality outside the chamber, the world of fact, as contrasted with the world of feeling and dream he is leaving, we find the misgivings justified. For once he is really outside, he finds himself confronted by "a black, impenetrable nothingness, as though heaven and all its lights were blotted from the system of the universe. It is as if Nature were dead . . ."

A "dead" Nature was of course the specter conjured up by nineteenth-century naturalism, the conception of a purposeless, valueless, colorless world, a "charnel house" world, faced by Ishmael at the end of the chapter on the whiteness of the whale in *Moby Dick*. Melville, we have long known, stared in fascinated horror at this vision of an "alien universe," stared at it more fixedly and with greater philosophic rigor than Hawthorne did. But one of the uses of this sketch is to remind us that Hawthorne was very much aware of what Melville was looking at, even though both his way of looking and what he finally saw were different from Melville's.

Here, for instance, the speaker, though at first plunged into a Slough of Despond, soon finds that there are various kinds of lights in what had at first seemed an unbroken darkness. Some of the lights are deceptive or illusory, especially if they are so bright that they seem utterly to dispel the darkness, but others are real and trustworthy. As the speaker continues his "plunge into the night," he discovers a way of distinguishing the false lights from the true: any light which makes men "forget the impenetrable obscurity that hems them in, and that can be dispelled only by radiance from above," is certain to be illusory.

Like Wallace Stevens a century later, who proposed to create a "skeptical music," Hawthorne is talking here at once about art and about life. He is proposing a life test for art's truth, without at all suggesting that the artist should abdicate, leaving "fact" and Nature in control. The internal world, the chamber of the heart where imagination operates freely, the world of dream, is the peculiar realm of the artist, and Hawthorne returns to it after his excursion into an apparently meaningless external reality has served its purpose. But the internal world is embedded in an external world, which it may ignore only at its peril. The imagination must remain responsible, even while it guards its freedom. No mere daydreaming will do. The romancer, Hawthorne wrote of himself elsewhere, need not aim at "a very minute fidelity" to history and nature, but he "sins unpardonably" if he violates "the truth of the human heart."

Irresponsible daydream, responsible imagination, fact without meaning, or even destructive of meaning — all are present and played against each other in this sketch. The center of Hawthorne's interest is, to be sure, elsewhere, in the moral and religious meanings which, with his usual emphasis, he makes explicit at the end. (Having encountered a figure with a lantern that casts its light in a "circular pattern," Hawthorne concludes, "This figure shall supply me with a moral . . . thus we, night wanderers through a stormy and dismal world, if we bear the lamp of Faith, enkindled at a celestial fire, it will surely lead us home to that heaven whence its radiance was borrowed.")

But the aesthetic meanings are here too, implicitly. No over-reading is required to see them. It was as a "dreamer," with insufficient experience of the world, Hawthorne says several times elsewhere, that he produced his tales and sketches during his apprentice years. But even while he dreamed and created, he was dissatisfied with dreaming. He wanted to test his dreams against a reality he could not control, to determine their truth.

When, in the Preface to *The House of the Seven Gables*, Hawthorne made his famous distinction between the novel and the romance, he was not at all intending to assign "truth" to the novel and mere "fantasy," or escapist dreaming, to the romance. He was distinguishing between "fact" (which the novel deals with) and "truth" (which is the province of the romance), and at the same time suggesting an orientation in which "fact" is external and "truth" internal. So far as he was defending, implicitly, the validity of his own practice as a romancer, he was implying a "mere" before "fact." (He was ambivalent about this, as he so often was on other matters, to be sure. He thought Emerson *too* idealistic, and he greatly admired the "beef and ale" realism of Trollope.)

The romantic artist creates, Hawthorne thought, by transforming fact into symbol, that is, into *meaningful* fact. Facts that he cannot see as meaningful may be disregarded. He is at liberty to manipulate his materials, to shape them freely into meaningful patterns, so long as he does not violate the truth of the human heart. Hawthorne felt that he himself could pursue his desired truth best by a combination of looking within and exercising the kind of imaginative sympathy that had been both his subject and his method in "The Old Apple Dealer." In a very suggestive metaphor in the Preface to *The Snow Image and Other Twice-Told Tales* in 1851, he defined his role as artist as that of "a person, who has been burrowing, to his utmost ability, into the depths of our common nature, for the purposes of psychological romance — and who pursues his researches in that dusky region, as he needs must, as well by the tact of sympathy as by the light of observation . . ."

After 1850 Hawthorne wrote no more tales or sketches and consistently belittled the ones he had written. He wondered, once, what he had ever meant by these "blasted allegories." Yet several of his earliest tales are among his best. "My Kinsman, Major Molineux," first printed in 1832, is surely one of the finest short stories in the language. Again and again in recent years critics have turned back to it and found new meanings — and no wonder, for its images are archetypal.

The vehicle for its themes is the journey from country to city, from simplicity and innocence to complexity and experience. Young Robin makes the journey to enlist the aid of a powerful kinsman, who will, he hopes, help him to "rise in the world." Armed only with a club, his innocence, and his native shrewdness, he is mysteriously baffled in his search for Major Molineux. He finds the city a bewildering and threatening place. Everything is ambiguous. Cruelty appears in the guise of patriotism and lust calls out in a "sweet voice" that seems to speak "Gospel truth." Symbols of authority have no power and epiphanies of meaning go unrecognized. To those already initiated, he is the object of ridicule, but he cannot discover the reason for the laughter that follows him through the streets as though he were having a bad dream.

When he finally rests beside a church after his long "evening of ambiguity and weariness," he sees, inside, a Bible illuminated by a ray of moonlight. He has remembered his father in their country home "holding the Scriptures in the golden light that fell from the western clouds." Nature and Scripture, General and Special Revelation, are united here, Hawthorne suggests, in presenting a way out of Robin's impasse. But Robin himself does not make the connection. Fortunately, a kindly stranger appears at this point, offers helpful advice, and finally tells Robin that "perhaps, as you are a shrewd youth, you may rise in the world without the help of your kinsman, Major Molineux." But this hope is offered only after Robin has taken his place in mankind's brotherhood in guilt by joining in the mob's ridicule of his Tory kinsman, thus repudiating the father-figure.

The reader feels that Robin may indeed rise, though not by means of his club, his innocence, or his shrewdness. His club has of course only made him ridiculous: one does not force one's way through moral and psychological initiations. His innocence is more fancied than real. Of it one might say what Hawthorne wrote in "Fancy's Show Box," that "Man must not disclaim his brotherhood, even with the guiltiest . . . Penitence must kneel." His shrewdness, if it is without love, can only alienate him, as a merely intellectual development made Ethan Brand lose his hold of "the magnetic chain of humanity." The kindly stranger is being gently ironic when he refers to Robin's shrewdness.

The ultimate reason why Robin's shrewdness is not enough for him to rely on is that man, as Hawthorne made clear in "The Old Apple Dealer," is not a machine. He has a soul. He therefore cannot be understood, Hawthorne believes, by empirical reason or observation alone. At the very center of his being there is a mystery, which will always remain a mystery, never be "solved," for, in Gabriel Marcel's terms, it is a mystery and not a problem. In the last analysis, what baffled Robin in his quest, before the kindly stranger came to his aid, is the same thing that made Hawthorne confess failure in his effort wholly to capture in words the essence of the old apple dealer.

The moonlit Bible in the church in "My Kinsman" may be related to the man with the lantern and to the "radiance from above" in "Beneath an Umbrella." The tin lantern is an analogue of the "lamp of Faith" which will lead us home to heaven just because its radiance is not of our creation but "borrowed" from heaven itself. There are two tests, apparently, for the validity of the various lights that appear in a dark world, their source and their effect. About the test by effect, Hawthorne is explicit: if a light is bright enough to seem to make the darkness disappear entirely, it is false — its effect depends upon a bedazzling of the eyes. The test by source he leaves to implication in his conclusion, but the implication is clear enough. The stranger's light will lead him home to his fireside because it was kindled there. "Just so" our faith will lead us back to its source. The light cast by the fire on the family hearth is our best analogue of the supernatural light that must guide us to an ultimate home. It images the light that art cannot picture more directly.

The sketch and the story reinforce each other on this matter. If Robin is not to become another Goodman Brown, overwhelmed by the discovery of evil, he must salvage something of his childhood faith. The vision of the moonlit Bible in the church and the appearance of the stranger who comes to his aid combine to suggest that he will do so once he ceases to rely solely on himself to save himself — on his innocence, his strength, and his shrewdness. Justification by faith, not by works, is implied — by a mature faith, a tested and tried faith that does not deny the darkness or ignore the complexity of the world.

If Robin's adventures in town had ended before he arrived at the church and met the friendly stranger, his story would have been one of simple loss with no compensating gain — a fall with no rise, an initiation into evil with no accompanying redefinition of the good. But Robin at the end has not been destroyed by the loss of his innocence. Indeed, he seems to be the better for it.

Could his case be taken as a paradigm for mankind? Could the Fall of Man be conceived as fortunate? On the whole, most of the time, Hawthorne thought so; or at least hoped so. But part of the time he could not summon so much hope. And he was aware of dangers involved in pursuing a line of thought that might seem to suggest that sin was beneficial. Taking as instructive myth what his ancestors had taken as literal history, he turned the subject around and around, examining it from every angle.

Of his four completed novels, only the last treats the subject directly. *The Marble Faun* is Hawthorne's theological novel. But *The Blithedale Romance* explicitly examines the possibility of undoing the Fall, and *The House of the Seven Gables* retells the story as enacted by a family over generations. Only *The Scarlet Letter* is not concerned with it. It simply assumes it. But even it adumbrates the familiar pattern: a clear fall into sin, followed by an ambiguous rise.

The Scarlet Letter is the perfect expression of what Roy Male has called "Hawthorne's tragic vision." There is light in this story as well as darkness, clarity as well as ambiguity — a symbolic rose in the first chapter as well as a cemetery and a prison. But the "radiance from above" never reaches the center of the action to save, to rescue, to guide home. The saintly Mr. Wilson walks by the scaffold carrying a lantern like that carried by the man of faith in "Beneath an Umbrella," but the light he sheds about him has no such effect on Dimmesdale as the stranger's light has on the speaker in the sketch. Hester's dark glossy hair shines in the sunlight as though it were surmounted by a halo, making her almost an image of "the divine maternity"; but the Puritans look at her only as an adulteress, and the reader is likely to feel that she is only a suffering woman. Though the novel shows us good coming out of evil, it shows it coming only at a tragic cost.

Hester, the "woman taken in adultery," rises to saintliness as she becomes an "angel of mercy" to the community, but her dreams of a new order of society can find no expression in her life and resignation is all she has to take the place of happiness. Few of us would envy her "rise." Or Dimmesdale's. In a novel constructed of ironic reversals, the apparently saintly minister first falls into a life of utter falsehood, then finally — too late, too late — rises toward integrity and truth until, in the final scaffold scene, the allusions to the death of Christ on the cross seem not wholly ironic. But there is no joy for Dimmesdale either, any more than there is for Hester. And though his faith is always assumed, it seems to have as its only consequence an intensification of his feeling of guilt. He is first cousin to Roderick Elliston in

"Egotism," the man with the snake in his stomach, so tormented by his morbid symptoms that he cannot forget himself.

The novel ends in a kind of gloomy Good Friday. The minister accepts the justice of his crucifixion, blesses his persecutors, and warns Hester not to expect fulfillment of their love in another life. The faith that earlier had chiefly served to increase his torment, now seems to afford him little basis for hope that his life has not been wasted. The light that feebly penetrates the gloom of the ending is of uncertain source — not from the hearth, certainly, and only obscurely "from above." The tombstone that serves the two graves of lovers separated in death as they were in life is lit "only by one ever-glowing point of light gloomier than the shadow." And what the dark light reveals as it strikes the words on the stone is the ambiguity not only of Hester's symbolic A (adulteress? angel?) but of the still dominant colors, red and black.

The red has been associated with nature and life and beauty — the rose beside the prison, Hester's vivid coloring, her beautiful needlework — but also with sin. Black has been associated with both sin and death — the prison and the cemetery. Hester and Arthur have not been able to escape the consequences of their past. There is very little here to relieve what Hawthorne calls in his first chapter "the darkening close of a tale of human frailty and sorrow." No wonder he resolved to make his next novel a happier one.

The chief problem facing the critic of *The House of the Seven Gables* today is presented precisely by his happy ending. Almost all modern readers have found it unconvincing, for a number of reasons. Phoebe and Holgrave fall in love, for one thing, rather abruptly. We see too little of them as lovers to believe fully in the reality of their love, and so in its redemptive power, as we must if we are to find Hawthorne's theme fully achieved. Then too, we may have trouble believing in their love because we have trouble believing in *them*. The portrayal of Phoebe is likely to strike us as a little sentimental: she moves too quickly from being an attractive country girl to being a symbol of Grace. Holgrave is better. Certainly he is very interesting theoretically as a portrait of the young American, pragmatic, oriented toward the future, full of energy and boundless hope, confident that he can control his destiny, a self-reliant secular utopian in effect. Yet for most readers he seems to have proved more interesting as a symbol than convincing as a character.

The marriage of Phoebe and Holgrave is the symbolic union of heart and head. Hawthorne associates the conservatism of the heart not only with the feminine but with both Nature and Grace. The ringlets of Phoebe's shining hair and the curves of her figure are related to the cycles of Nature's annual death and renewal exhibited in the elm that overshadows the house. The radicalism of the head, of reason, that leads Holgrave to expect uninterrupted progress, is associated equally with the fact of decline and the dream of easy progress without suffering. Rejecting the paradox of life through death suggested by the flowers growing in an angle of the rotting roof, rationalism oversimplifies history in its reading of both past and future. For all his "futurism," Holgrave is in a sense more closely linked to the past than Phoebe is, for without her influence he would perpetuate the very errors that led to the long Pyncheon decline.

The Pyncheons have lived by the merely reasonable standards of a secular morality. For the sake of the world's goods, power and money, they have violated the heart's higher laws. The result has been self-defeating. Living by reason alone, they have planned and schemed shrewdly, but time and nature have defeated them. Clifford's mind is ruined and the dead judge sitting in the dark chamber will never execute his plans. Though he is at first morally neutral, Holgrave falsifies history, which is better expressed by images of circles than by straight lines, whether the lines are pictured as pointing downward or upward, suggesting uninterrupted decline or uninterrupted progress. He might have learned his lesson from the ancient elm, if he had been more sensitive to its meanings, as earlier Pyncheons might have learned the same lesson from "Alice's posies," but it takes his love for Phoebe to teach him what Clifford intuitively knows, that history neither endlessly repeats itself nor marches straight onward from novelty to novelty, but moves in an "ascending spiral curve."

But the heart can read such revelations, provided equally by Nature and Scripture, better than the mind, so it is not surprising that this first cousin to idealistic Aylmer and empirical Giovanni should need Phoebe to teach him. That he is so quickly taught is the surprising thing. One of the reasons the ending strikes the reader as unconvincing is that Holgrave puts up so little resistance to Phoebe's truths. The escape from the house and what it has stood for seems at last too easy.

What Hawthorne *meant* to suggest by his ending, though, is pretty clear, whether it works with us or not. The basic pattern is one of life, death, and resurrection or renewal. Within this cyclical pattern love acts redemptively, but not in the sense of removing one from the downward phase of the cycle. If love has its way, the inherited fortune and the fine new house in the suburbs will not bring about a pointless repetition of tragic Pyncheon history. We may legitimately hope that the circles of history include an upward movement to form a "spiral curve."

Just how difficult Hawthorne found it to maintain even so chastened a hope becomes apparent in his next novel. *The Blithedale Romance* assumes the Fall of man and examines the hope of undoing it, of returning to an unspoiled Eden or Arcadia by creating a pilot model of a better world. Blithedale is a socialistic colony in which the conditions that have prevailed since the Fall should prevail no more. It aspires to be a true community in which men will work together for the common good. The law of love will be put into effect in a practical way for perhaps the first time in human history. Man will no longer be shut in the prison of self.

But the project does not work out that way. This is Hawthorne's most hopeless novel. *The Scarlet Letter* was tragic, but this is simply cold. Coverdale, the narrator, is glad that he *once* hoped for a better world, but since experience has destroyed the hope, in effect he is saying that innocence is a happy state while it lasts, before the plunge into experience destroys it. The colonists at Blithedale were not united for the common good. Instead, each used the project for his own selfish purposes. Furthermore, the group as a whole found itself in a state of competition with the surrounding larger community. Not love and sharing and truth were dominant here but competition, mutual distrust, and masquerading.

Two patterns of imagery carry a great burden of the meaning in the novel, and both have the same effect thematically. Fire images suggest that warmth of the heart, that mutuality of hope that, if it could have been maintained (if indeed it was ever as real as it once seemed), *might* have made the venture succeed. But the great blazing fire on the hearth that warmed the hearts as well as the bodies of the colonists on the first night of Coverdale's stay burned out quickly: it was built merely of brushwood. Only ashes remain now, as Coverdale looks back at the experience, to remind him of generous hopes once entertained.

The other chief line of the dual image pattern is made up of various types of veils and disguises. As Hawthorne had said of Dimmesdale in *The Scarlet Letter* that at least one clear truth emerged from his complex and tragic story, "Be true! Be true!" so here he feels that if the colonists cannot "be true" with one another, cannot take off their several veils and disguises, there can be no real community. From the "Veiled Lady" of the opening chapter, who would *like* to take off her veil; to Coverdale, whose name suggests covering the valley of the heart and who spends much of his time observing people from behind a screen of leaves or window curtains; to Old Moodie, with the patch over his eye and his false name; to Westervelt with his false teeth and Zenobia with her artificial flowers — all the chief characters are in some way masked. Until they take off their masks, revealing themselves to each other in love and truth, no such venture as theirs can succeed, Hawthorne implies. Since instead of unveiling themselves they masquerade throughout the novel, there is no real hope in their enterprise, generous and idealistic though it once seemed.

But of course if, as Hawthorne was to write later about the Civil War, "No human effort . . . has ever yet resulted according to the purpose of its projectors," then the venture was doomed from the start, whether or not the reformers managed to take off their veils. Hawthorne does not resolve this ambiguity, and it is one of the sources of our sense that this is his most hopeless novel. If we take the veils to mean only that which hides man from man, then there may be hope that a sufficient number of personal conversions may ultimately result in a better world: what no merely external changes can do, an inner change may effect. Utopianism may be mistaken, but individuals do change, and if enough of them change . . .

With this reading, the final meaning of the novel is not far from the meaning of "Earth's Holocaust." A better world required better people, a change in the *heart*: "unless they hit upon some method of purifying that foul cavern, forth from it will reissue all the shapes of wrong and misery — the same old shapes or worse ones — which they have taken such a vast deal of trouble to consume to ashes."

But perhaps what is ultimately veiled is an intolerable reality. If so, this "exploded scheme for beginning the life of Paradise anew," this effort to reverse man's mythic history and undo the Fall, was doomed before it began, before Coverdale "plunged into the heart of the pitiless snow-storm, in quest of a better life." At times the "wintry snow-storm roaring in the chimney" at Blithedale seems more real to Coverdale than the "chill mockery of a fire" that is all his memory retains to keep hope alive. The outside darkness and cold may *be* reality, the brushwood fire itself a kind of veiling delusion, necessary if we are to have hope but none the less false.

Such a reading would make the meaning of the novel equivalent to what the meaning of "Beneath an Umbrella" would have been if the speaker had stopped just outside his door, with the discovery of a Nature seemingly dead, and had not gone on through the dark to find at last a true light. Dream and reality, the light and the darkness were, finally, not utterly at odds in the sketch. In the novel they may be. Neither Coverdale, at any rate, nor the reader, can quite dispose of the suspicion that they are.

By the time Hawthorne came, a few years later, to write his last completed novel, he was ready to confront directly the subject he had treated implicitly so often before. *The Marble Faun* is, as the dark mysterious Miriam says, "the story of the fall of man." In it Donatello, who has grown up in innocence in a kind of rural Eden or Arcadia, is, like Robin before him, introduced to sin in the city. Like Robin, too, who had joined in the cruel laughter of the mob, Donatello is corrupted by what he encounters among art students in Rome. He commits a murder, though his intentions are obscure and his provocation great. Like Robin, finally, he is matured by the experience, brought from an innocence that was only half human at best to a condition in which he shares mankind's nature and lot.

Was the fall then "fortunate"? Miriam poses the question and implies a hopeful answer: " 'The story of the fall of man! Is it not repeated in our romance of Monte Beni? And may we follow the analogy yet further? Was that very sin — into which Adam precipitated himself and all his race, — was it the destined means by which, over a long pathway of toil and sorrow, we are to attain a higher, brighter, and profounder happiness, than our lost birthright gave?' "

We must suppose, I think, that Hawthorne intended his reader to answer Miriam's question in the affirmative and that he further intended this answer to be the largest meaning of his novel. But if this was his intention, he was only partially successful in embodying it. Hilda, the blonde New England maiden, comes down from the tower of her spotless innocence, to be sure, to marry the coolly detached sculptor Kenyon, and he is presumably humanized by his love for her. But this union of heart and head is not much more convincing as a symbol of redemptive possibilities than the similar marriage of Phoebe and Holgrave in *The House of the Seven Gables*; and for the two chief actors in the plot — Kenyon and Hilda are onlookers, affected by what they see — there is no promise of happiness. Donatello, the archetypal man, ends in prison, isolated not only from Miriam but from mankind by his sin. Only in some figurative or purely spiritual sense has he been drawn into Hawthorne's *brotherhood* of sin. And for Miriam, the most thoroughly created and felt character in the novel, there is even less assurance of happiness than Hawthorne granted Hester.

In short, though the intended meaning of the novel may be reasonably clear — a qualified affirmation, of the kind consistent with a tragic but not hopeless view of life — the achieved meaning is obscure. We end convinced of the loss of innocence, and of the present reality of the "long pathway of toil and sorrow," but the evidence that this pathway may lead to "a higher, brighter, and profounder happiness" falls far short of being convincing — to us, and, I suspect, to Hawthorne himself at this stage in his life.

The qualified happy ending of "My Kinsman" was much more convincing, and the ending of "Roger Malvin's Burial" is clearer. The meaning of the latter tale is comparable to what we may take to be the intended meaning in the novel, that suffering and sacrifice are the only means to redemptive reunion with God and man, but there is nothing in the tale, as there is in the novel, to make us doubt the validity of that meaning. In *The Marble Faun* Hawthorne leaned principally upon Hilda with her spotless heart to provide hope. She proved a weak reed.

Hawthorne has never been wholly out of favor since the publication of *The Scarlet Letter*, but in the half century following his death he seemed much more old-fashioned than he does now. In a period of literary realism his symbolic and allegorical fiction seemed to need defense: it was not clear that it was a valid way of writing. Even James patronized him and could generally think of no better way of praising the pieces he liked best than to call them "charming."

Both literary, and philosophical and religious, changes since James's day have made it quite unnecessary to apologize for or defend either Hawthorne's mode of writing or his vision. When he failed, as of course he often did, it was sometimes because he had, for the time being, succeeded too well in becoming the "man of society" he always wanted to be — had too successfully adjusted himself to his age, come to share both its mode of feeling and its opinions too uncritically. His blonde maidens are a case in point. Reflecting the mid-century idealization of woman and wholly inconsistent with his own otherwise persistent and consistent idea of mankind's brotherhood in guilt, they remain, fortunately, on the fringes of the action in *The Scarlet Letter* but weaken *The House of the Seven Gables* when they move into center in the person of Phoebe.

But even his failures are more interesting than most writers' successes. His probings into the nature and consequences of guilt and alienation sometimes struck earlier generations as morbid, but we have been prepared to understand them by Camus and Sartre and Kafka. His explorations of the possibilities of redemptive reunion need no defense in an age when philosophers have popularized the term *engagement*.

The scene in *The House of the Seven Gables* when Clifford attempts to join the procession in the street by jumping through the arched window suggests both Existential philosophy and antirealist fictional practice. Hawthorne's terms *head* and *heart* may sound a little old-fashioned, but his constant implication that the realities they stand for must interpenetrate and balance each other is as modern as psychoanalysis. His characteristic way of treating moral matters with the kind of ambiguity that makes both the psychological and the moral or religious perspectives on them relevant, the two perspectives quite distinct yet neither canceling the other, is likely to seem a major virtue to an age determined to assert the reality of man's freedom and responsibility, yet almost overwhelmingly conscious of the mechanisms of conditioning.

We are prepared today even for his special blend and alternation of light and darkness. Tillich and the religious Existentialists have taught us enough about the dynamics of faith to enable us to respond naturally to a writer who explored the darkness to the very limits of the town searching for a trustworthy light. Perhaps no nineteenth-century American writer today seems so likely to reward rereading as Hawthorne.

✃ Selected Bibliography

Principal Works of Nathaniel Hawthorne

AN EDITION of the complete works intended to be definitive is in preparation by the Ohio State University Press, edited by William Charvat, Roy H. Pearce, and others. Until it becomes available the standard complete editions are the Riverside Edition, 12 vols. (Boston: Houghton, Mifflin, 1883), and the Old Manse Edition, 22 vols. (1904).

Fanshawe. Boston: Marsh and Capen, 1828.

Twice-Told Tales. Boston: American Stationers Co., 1837. Second series, Boston: James Monroe, 1842.

Mosses from an Old Manse. New York: Wiley and Putnam, 1846.

The Scarlet Letter. Boston: Ticknor, Reed, and Fields, 1850.

The House of the Seven Gables. Boston: Ticknor, Reed, and Fields, 1851.

The Snow-Image and Other Twice-Told Tales. Boston: Ticknor, Reed, and Fields, 1851.

The Blithedale Romance. Boston: Ticknor, Reed, and Fields, 1852.

The Life of Franklin Pierce. Boston: Ticknor, Reed, and Fields, 1852.

A Wonder Book for Girls and Boys. Boston: Ticknor, Reed, and Fields, 1852.

Tanglewood Tales for Girls and Boys. Boston: Ticknor, Reed, and Fields, 1853.

The Marble Faun. Boston: Ticknor and Fields, 1860.

Our Old Home. Boston: Ticknor and Fields, 1863.

Passages from the American Note-Books, edited by Sophia Hawthorne. Boston: Ticknor and Fields, 1868. (*The American Notebooks*, edited by Randall Stewart. New Haven: Yale University Press, 1932.)

Passages from the English Note-Books, edited by Sophia Hawthorne. Boston: Fields, Osgood, 1870. (*The English Notebooks*, edited by Randall Stewart. New York: Modern Language Association, 1941.)

Dr. Grimshawe's Secret, edited by Julian Hawthorne. Boston: Osgood, 1883. (*Hawthorne's Dr. Grimshawe's Secret*, edited by Edward H. Davidson. Cambridge, Mass.: Harvard University Press, 1954.)

Hawthorne as Editor: Selections from His Writings in the American Magazine of Useful and Entertaining Knowledge, edited by Arlin Turner. Baton Rouge: Louisiana State University Press, 1941.

Current American Reprints

The Blithedale Romance. New York: Dell. $.75. New York: Dolphin (Double-day). $.95.

The Complete Novels and Selected Tales of Nathaniel Hawthorne, edited by Norman Holmes Pearson. New York: Modern Library (Random House). $2.95.

Hawthorne's Short Stories, edited by Newton Arvin. New York: Vintage (Random House). $1.25.

The House of the Seven Gables. New York: Dell. $.50. New York: Dolphin. $.95. New York: Signet (New American Library). $.50. New York: Washington Square Press. $.45.

The Marble Faun. New York: Dell. $.50. New York: Dolphin. $.95. New York: Pocket Books. $.35. New York. Signet. $.50.

Nathaniel Hawthorne: Selected Tales and Sketches, edited by Hyatt H. Waggoner. New York: Rinehart Editions. $.95.

The Scarlet Letter. New York: Collier. $.65. New York: Dell. $.50. New York: Dolphin. $.95. New York: Modern Library College Edition. $.65. New York: Signet. $.50. New York: Washington Square Press. $.45.

Twice-Told Tales and Other Short Stories. New York: Washington Square Press. $.50.

Bibliographical Aids

Browne, Nina E. *A Bibliography of Nathaniel Hawthorne.* Boston: Houghton, Mifflin, 1905.

Cathcart, Wallace H. *Bibliography of the Works of Nathaniel Hawthorne.* Cleveland: Rowfant Club, 1905.

Fogle, R. H. Bibliography in *Hawthorne's Fiction: The Light and the Dark.* Norman: University of Oklahoma Press, 1952. (The bibliography at the back of this book is the best available for literary critical purposes.)

Gross, Seymour L. *A "Scarlet Letter" Handbook.* San Francisco: Wadsworth, 1960. (A full and well-selected bibliography on this novel.)

Spiller, Robert E., and others, eds. *Literary History of the United States,* vol. 3. New York: Macmillan, 1948. *Supplement,* edited by Richard M. Ludwig, 1959.

Critical and Biographical Studies

Arvin, Newton. *Hawthorne.* Boston: Little, Brown, 1929.

Bridge, Horatio. *Personal Recollections of Nathaniel Hawthorne.* New York: Harper, 1893.

Fogle, Richard H. *Hawthorne's Fiction: The Light and the Dark.* Norman: University of Oklahoma Press, 1952.

Hawthorne, Julian. *Nathaniel Hawthorne and His Wife.* Boston: Osgood, 1885.
_____. *Hawthorne and His Circle.* New York: Harper, 1903.
Hoeltje, Hubert H. *Inward Sky: The Mind and Heart of Nathaniel Hawthorne.* Durham: Duke University Press, 1962.
James, Henry. *Hawthorne.* London: Macmillan, 1879.
Lathrop, G. P. *A Study of Hawthorne.* Boston: Osgood, 1876.
Lathrop, Rose Hawthorne. *Memories of Hawthorne.* Boston: Houghton, Mifflin, 1897.
Loggins, Vernon. *The Hawthornes: The Story of Seven Generations of an American Family.* New York: Columbia University Press, 1951.
Male, Roy R. *Hawthorne's Tragic Vision.* Austin: University of Texas Press, 1957.
Stewart, Randall. *Nathaniel Hawthorne: A Biography.* New Haven: Yale University Press, 1948.
Turner, Arlin. *Nathaniel Hawthorne: An Introduction and Interpretation.* New York: Barnes and Noble, 1961.
Van Doren, Mark. *Nathaniel Hawthorne: A Critical Biography.* New York: Sloane, 1949.
Wagenknecht, Edward. *Nathaniel Hawthorne: Man and Writer.* New York: Oxford University Press, 1961.
Waggoner, Hyatt H. *Hawthorne: A Critical Study.* Cambridge, Mass.: Harvard University Press, 1955.

Books Containing Chapters on Hawthorne

Bewley, Marius. *The Complex Fate.* London: Chatto and Windus, 1952.
_____. *The Eccentric Design: Form in the Classic American Novel.* New York: Columbia University Press, 1959.
Feidelson, Charles, Jr. *Symbolism and American Literature.* Chicago: University of Chicago Press, 1953.
Hoffman, Daniel G. *Form and Fable in American Fiction.* New York: Oxford University Press, 1961.
Levin, Harry. *The Power of Blackness: Hawthorne, Poe, Melville.* New York: Knopf, 1958.
Lewis, R. W. B. *The American Adam: Innocence, Tragedy, and Tradition in the Nineteenth Century.* Chicago: University of Chicago Press, 1955.
Matthiessen, F. O. *American Renaissance.* New York: Oxford University Press, 1941.
Stewart, Randall. *American Literature and Christian Doctrine.* Baton Rouge: Louisiana State University Press, 1958.
Warren, Austin. *Rage for Order.* Chicago: University of Chicago Press, 1948.
Winters, Yvor. *In Defense of Reason.* New York: Swallow Press and Morrow, 1947.